JOYCE POWZYK

TASMANIA
A WILDLIFE JOURNEY

Lothrop, Lee & Shepard Books
New York

This book was first conceived on an arduous hike through Tasmania and developed while I was involved in an environmental protest. I would like to thank Elsbeth deVlaming, Hunter Shannonhouse, Doug Decker, and Jim Gates, with whom I shared these experiences. Stephen Henri Devoto and my editor, Barbara Lalicki, gave me the unending support needed to complete this project.

The authoritative source for species and subspecies names used herein is *The Australian Museum Complete Book of Australian Mammals,* edited by Ronald Strahan, published in 1983 by Angus & Robertson.

Library of Congress Cataloging in Publication Data
Powzyk, Joyce Ann.   Tasmania, a wildlife journey.
Summary: Presents in text and illustrations, the wildlife observed by the author on a journey through the island of Tasmania. 1. Zoology—Australia—Tasmania—Juvenile literature. [1. Zoology—Australia—Tasmania] I. Title.
QL339.T2P68   1987   599.09946   86-7288
ISBN 0-688-06459-0   ISBN 0-688-06460-4 (lib. bdg.)

Printed in Japan
The cover shows a native cat; a Tasmanian wombat is pictured on the title page.
10 9 8 7 6 5 4 3 2 1   First Edition

This book is dedicated to
the Tasmanian Wolf
that once flourished on the island of Tasmania.

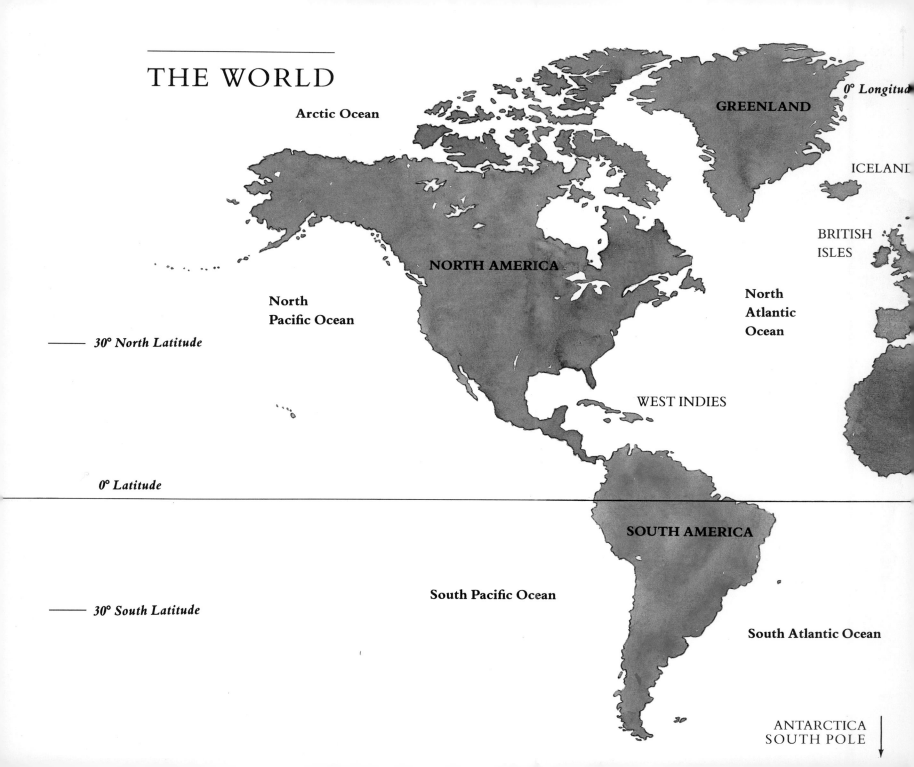

THE WORLD

Arctic Ocean

GREENLAND

0° Longitud

ICELANI

BRITISH
ISLES

NORTH AMERICA

North
Pacific Ocean

North
Atlantic
Ocean

30° North Latitude

WEST INDIES

0° Latitude

SOUTH AMERICA

South Pacific Ocean

30° South Latitude

South Atlantic Ocean

ANTARCTICA
SOUTH POLE

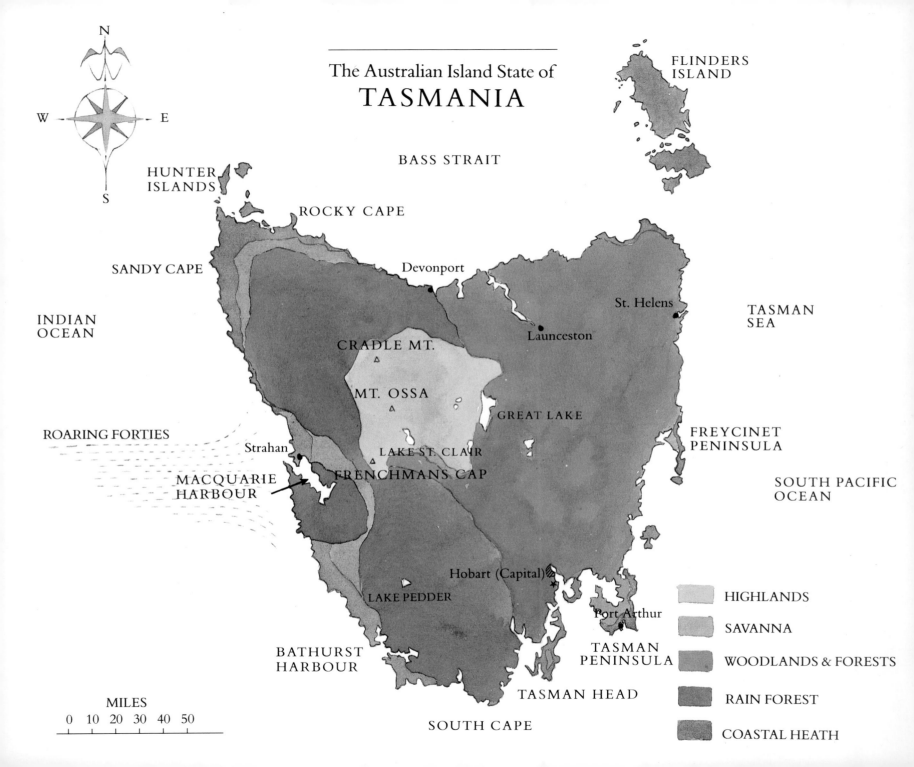

The Australian Island State of
TASMANIA

N
W — E
S

FLINDERS ISLAND

BASS STRAIT

HUNTER ISLANDS

ROCKY CAPE

SANDY CAPE

Devonport

St. Helens

TASMAN SEA

INDIAN OCEAN

CRADLE MT.

Launceston

MT. OSSA

GREAT LAKE

FREYCINET PENINSULA

ROARING FORTIES

Strahan

LAKE ST. CLAIR

FRENCHMANS CAP

SOUTH PACIFIC OCEAN

MACQUARIE HARBOUR

Hobart (Capital)

LAKE PEDDER

Port Arthur

TASMAN PENINSULA

BATHURST HARBOUR

TASMAN HEAD

SOUTH CAPE

MILES
0 10 20 30 40 50

HIGHLANDS

SAVANNA

WOODLANDS & FORESTS

RAIN FOREST

COASTAL HEATH

COME WITH ME AND VISIT A REMOTE ISLAND OFF THE coast of Australia. Few people travel to Tasmania, and even fewer have ever seen a Tasmanian devil or a tiger cat in the wild.

The island seems lost in time, almost prehistoric. Old volcanoes rise above the forests of tree ferns that are home to primitive plants and pouched marsupial animals. Tasmania's unique climate, landscape, and physical isolation have combined to produce species found nowhere else in the world.

We will take a wildlife journey through Tasmania, watching for the animals that live in each of its five different habitats. The adventure begins in the highlands and continues through the grassy savanna into sparse woodlands and on into thick, damp rain forest. It is springtime, and we travel for several days, ending our journey when we reach the windy coast. Some of the animals we will see are also found on the mainland, reminding us that Tasmania was once connected to Australia until it was separated by the rising waters of the South Pacific Ocean.

Our journey starts in the highlands on a cool, clear day. Even during the spring, storms move into these mountains without warning, and there is a fresh blanket of snow on the ground. Looming in the background are weathered volcanoes. *Black currawongs* watch us from the rocky outcrops.

A family of *Tasmanian wombats* push the new-fallen snow away
from the entrance to their sleeping burrow. *Little marsupial mice* are
searching for frozen insects in the drifts. We pass snow gum trees
that have grown gnarled and twisted by wind. Their bark is
bright against the snow.

A *copperhead snake* is sunning itself on the rocky path that leads us down from the highlands into the grassy savanna. The markings of this poisonous snake make it difficult to spot in the grass. It slithers away and soon disappears. Soaring overhead is a *wedge-tailed eagle*, closely watching its vast domain. A pair of *Tasmanian echidnas* are busy in the tussock grass, catching ants with their long, sticky tongues.

Dragonflies patrol the air over large cushion plants that are composed entirely of moss. Two *Tasmanian pademelons* are feeding in the bush. One has a heavy pouch because she is carrying a baby. She thumps her foot to warn other pademelons of our presence.

We continue through the dense scrub and gradually move into woodlands. A *Tasmanian native hen* walks through the undergrowth, flicking her tail while clucking softly. The sound of gurgling water leads us to a stream that emerges from a rock face to form a small waterfall. As we stop here to rest, *welcome swallows* swoop by, picking off young insects that have emerged from their larval stage in the stream.

A shy *Tasmanian bettong* hops into view. It rises up on its hind legs,
sniffing the air for danger. The bettong then gathers a clump of
dry grass with its forelegs and places the grass in its curled tail.
This new bundle will be added to its nest. A noisy group of *green
rosellas* flocks into a blue gum tree. The bettong vanishes,
frightened by the birds' loud chattering.

We follow the stream as it flows into a pond. Several large *black swans* live here with their young, which are called cygnets. These graceful birds arch their necks as they slowly glide across the water. A *water rat* catches our attention as it jumps into the pond with a splash. The rat uses its semi-webbed feet to swim after a water beetle.

The screeching calls of *sulphur-crested cockatoos* pierce the silence. The cockatoos fly through a cluster of Huon pine trees on the way to their distant feeding grounds. We spot a small bird, colored bright blue and orange, on the far side of the pond. It is an *azure kingfisher*. The bird dives headfirst into the water, reappearing with a small minnow clamped in its bill.

As we walk along, the trees suddenly become more numerous and the air feels heavy and damp. The sparse woodlands have given way to thick rain forest. A growling black animal with a white V across its chest is pacing up and down the far stream bank. Snarling, it jumps into the water to retrieve a dead fish. The animal devours food, crunching bones with its strong jaws. This is a *Tasmanian devil*, a fierce scavenger that also hunts.

Ignoring the noisy devil, a group of *yellow-tailed black cockatoos* quietly feeds on grubs from beneath the bark of eucalyptus trees. A poisonous *tiger snake* glides across the ground. It is about to raid a nest of *beautiful firetails* in the lower tree branches. The rain forest is full of life; every plant and animal has its own niche.

Night is falling, and the large tree ferns cast dark shadows. A soft rain begins to fall, and its patter echoes throughout the forest. Two *musk lorikeets* settle down to sleep under a sheltering branch. The night seems peaceful, but some animals have just awakened. A *native cat* appears, sniffing through the wet leaves for the scent of a mouse or bird. The cat suddenly smells something and dashes off to continue its nightly hunt.

A *boobook owl* calls from a tree. Over and over the owl repeats its name, *Boobook, Boobook,* challenging any other boobook owl to come near. From our hiding place we glimpse a *barred bandicoot* with dark stripes across its rump. It starts to dig up a witchetty grub, or beetle larva, and is immediately joined by two small bandicoots. The young snatch the food from their mother and eagerly look for more.

Darting between the trees, an *owlet nightjar* flies after a large gum moth. Startled, the bandicoots gallop off into the bush, causing a shower of raindrops to fall. *Pygmy-possums* are moving through the forest. They jump from branch to branch and flower to flower, feeding on the sweet nectar of Tasmanian black peppermint trees.

Breaking through the brush comes a *tiger cat* with spots on its back and tail. The tiger cat is the largest carnivore on Tasmania except for the *Tasmanian wolf*, which may be extinct. The cat climbs a nearby tree and easily catches a sleeping parrot. In a burst of feathers and squawks, the other birds fly off to look for a safe roosting area.

The approaching dawn colors the sky a light gray. The rain has finally stopped. We pass a cave where *lesser long-eared bats* are returning from their nightly hunt for insects. Also returning is a *ringtail possum* with a young one clinging to her back. The possum's curled tail grasps the smaller branches and helps support her heavy load as she climbs to her nest.

Hidden in the bushes are several large *forester kangaroos*. They watch us cautiously, ready to flee if alarmed. We move on past a *blotched blue-tongued lizard* that suns itself on a rock. Nearby, *yellow wattlebirds* feed on the flowers of a banksia tree. When a wattlebird comes too close, the lizard opens its mouth and threatens the bird with its bright tongue.

As we near the coast, rain forest gives way to coastal heath and bracken. Dozing beneath a bottlebrush tree are several *Bennett's wallabies*. Their fur is long and thick because Tasmania can get very cold. *New Holland honeyeaters* hang upside down, probing the flowers for nectar. Suddenly we hear an animal moving through the brush, hot on the wallabies' trail. Perhaps it is the rare Tasmanian wolf.

This species was last seen in the wild in 1930, when a wolf was tracked by a hunter. The wallabies sense the danger and bolt through the undergrowth. We can hear their loud thumps as they hop away. The hidden animal breathes deeply, sniffing the ground for the scent of its prey. Finally the bushes rustle, and then there is silence. We will never know if this was a Tasmanian wolf.

We slowly continue our journey and flush a covey of *bronzewing pigeons.* Their wings whistle as they rise into the air. Several *Australian fur-seals* are resting on the beach. They notice us and roll their large brown eyes in our direction. A thick-necked male roars a warning as two females from his harem disappear into the water.

As we walk toward the shore, a gusty breeze blows sand in our faces, and we smell the salt and seaweed. *Australian gannets* fly overhead on long, tapered wings. Our journey ends at the coastline that encircles this island. With the now-distant mountains behind us, we gaze out over the Tasman Sea.

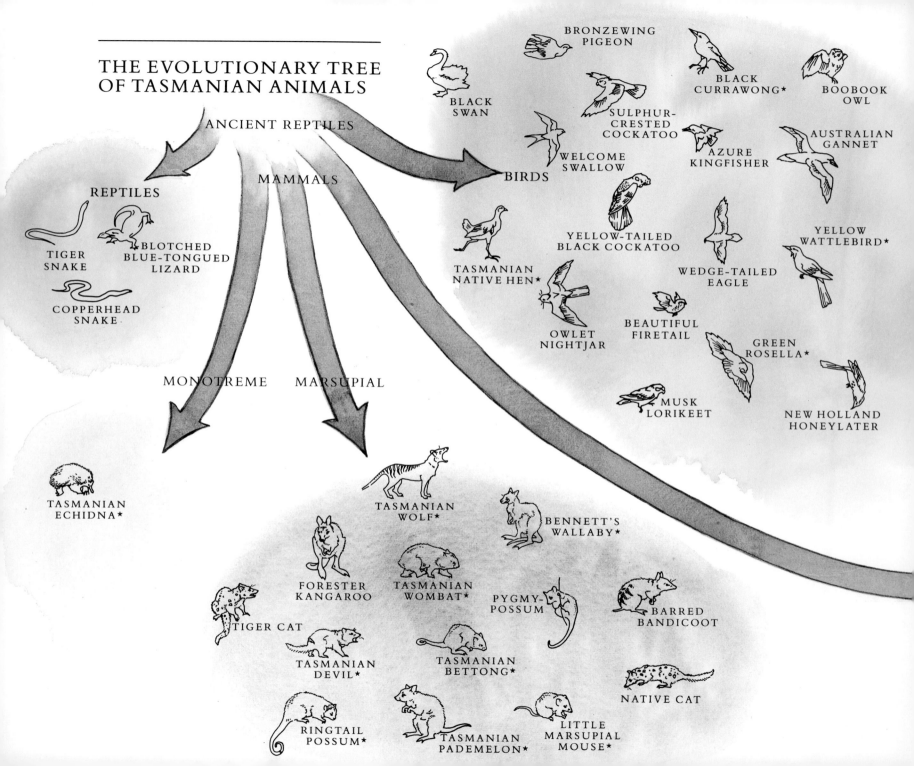

THE EVOLUTIONARY TREE OF TASMANIAN ANIMALS

ANCIENT REPTILES

MAMMALS

BIRDS

REPTILES

TIGER SNAKE

BLOTCHED BLUE-TONGUED LIZARD

COPPERHEAD SNAKE

MONOTREME

MARSUPIAL

TASMANIAN ECHIDNA★

BLACK SWAN

BRONZEWING PIGEON

SULPHUR-CRESTED COCKATOO

WELCOME SWALLOW

BLACK CURRAWONG★

BOOBOOK OWL

AZURE KINGFISHER

AUSTRALIAN GANNET

YELLOW-TAILED BLACK COCKATOO

WEDGE-TAILED EAGLE

YELLOW WATTLEBIRD★

TASMANIAN NATIVE HEN★

OWLET NIGHTJAR

BEAUTIFUL FIRETAIL

GREEN ROSELLA★

MUSK LORIKEET

NEW HOLLAND HONEYLATER

TASMANIAN WOLF★

BENNETT'S WALLABY★

FORESTER KANGAROO

TASMANIAN WOMBAT★

PYGMY-POSSUM

BARRED BANDICOOT

TIGER CAT

TASMANIAN DEVIL★

TASMANIAN BETTONG★

NATIVE CAT

RINGTAIL POSSUM★

TASMANIAN PADEMELON★

LITTLE MARSUPIAL MOUSE★

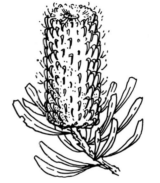

A Note on the Plant Life

Many Tasmanian plants are as primitive as the marsupial animals found in this island habitat. For example, the primitive species' means of propagation, in which spores and seeds are spread by the wind, has enabled both the ancient tree ferns and the Huon pine to exist successfully for 130 million years. The cushion plant is also unusual; it is a community of plants rather than a single individual. This plant is a moss that made the transition from a water to a land habitat; the dense community structure provides a way for the plant to retain its moisture. Also growing on the island are banksias belonging to the ancient plant family of Proteaceae, which appeared at about the same time as the first marsupials. The nectar of the beautiful cone-shaped banksia blossoms is an important food source for many Tasmanian animals.

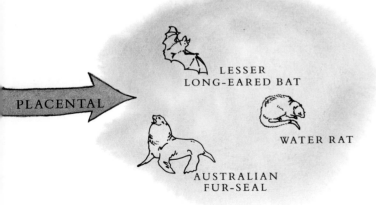

PLACENTAL

LESSER
LONG-EARED BAT

WATER RAT

AUSTRALIAN
FUR-SEAL

★ Asterisks indicate animal species or subspecies found only on the island of Tasmania.

GLOSSARY

BRACKEN: coarse ferns

BURROW: a hole dug into the ground by an animal for shelter

CARNIVORE: a flesh-eating animal

CLIMATE: the combined wind, moisture, and temperature of a region

COVEY: a small group of birds

CYGNET: a young swan

EVOLUTION: a process of development through which an organism has acquired its distinctive physical traits

EXTINCT: no longer existing

FORELEGS: front legs

GRUB: an early, wormlike form of an insect that will turn into an adult form

HABITAT: the physical environment where a plant or animal lives and finds its food

HAREM: a group of females controlled by a male

HEATH: an open area of land that is covered with coarse, short plant life because of its poor underlying soil

HIGHLAND: elevated or mountainous land where it is cold enough for snow to fall

ISLAND: a piece of land surrounded by water, smaller than the continents of Africa, Antarctica, Asia, Australia, Europe, North America, and South America.

LARVAL STAGE: the early period of development during which an animal has a self-supporting form that does not resemble its adult form

MAMMAL: a warm-blooded animal that is usually covered with hair and that suckles its young on nourishing milk

MARSUPIAL: a primitive mammal that gives birth to underdeveloped young, which are usually carried in a pouch where they feed on milk from the mother

MINNOW: a small fish

MONOTREME: a primitive, egg-laying mammal

NECTAR: the sweet liquid given off by certain flowers

NICHE: a specific habitat in which an animal or plant can find the food and shelter it needs to exist

PLACENTA: a connecting organ that nourishes the developing young inside the mother's body

PLACENTAL: a mammal with a placenta

PREY: an animal that is hunted as food

PRIMITIVE: belonging to or characteristic of an early and more simple stage of evolution

RAIN FOREST: a dense, leafy green forest with heavy rainfall

ROARING FORTIES: strong, wet, westerly winds located between 40 degrees and 50 degrees south latitude

ROOST: a place where birds rest

SAVANNA: an area of land covered with thick grasses and having few trees

SCAVENGER: an animal that will often eat dead or rotting food

SCRUB: thick, dense vegetation consisting of stunted trees and bushes

SEMIWEBBED FEET: feet with flaps of skin partially connecting the toes, useful for swimming

TUSSOCK GRASS: a type of grass that grows in compact tussocks, or tufts

UNDERGROWTH: low growth of plants on the forest floor

VOLCANO: a mountain that is formed by hot, liquid rock erupting from the earth's surface

WEATHERED: worn down from the effects of sun, rain, and wind; faded in color

WITCHETTY GRUB: a native Australian term for the larva of a beetle

WOODLAND: land covered with grass and many trees

After her stay in Australia, Joyce Powzyk was eager to see Tasmania, because an ancestor of hers, George Hobler, had been one of the island's nineteenth-century settlers.

The artist and naturalist spent weeks exploring and hiking in the island's wilderness. She also participated in a successful international protest against a proposed hydroelectric dam near Lake Pedder. This dam would have had a serious impact on Tasmania's beautiful and remote southwest rain forest.

Joyce Powzyk is employed as an artist at Rockefeller University in New York City and also works for the Jacques Cousteau Society. She continues to do natural history fieldwork in such places as eastern Africa and the island of Madagascar. She is the author of *Wallaby Creek*, a 1985 ALA Notable Book.